WORDS FROM A-Z

Written by M.C. Leeka
Illustrated by Chris McDonough

Modern Publishing
A Division of Unisystems, Inc.
New York, New York 10022

Aa Aa Aa

A is for apples
you bake in a pie.

A is for airplane
that flies in the sky.

A is for anchors
that hold ships in place.

A is for astronaut
who travels through space.

Bb Bb Bb

B is for balloons
you fill up with air.

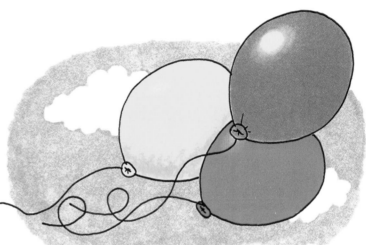

B is for barber
who cuts your hair.

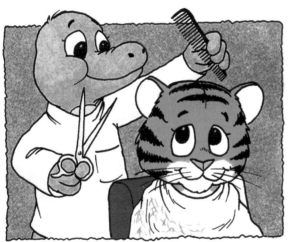

B is for boots
you wear on your feet.

B is for bus
that rolls down the street.

Cc Cc Cc

C is for candy
you buy at the store.

C is for carpet
that covers the floor.

C is for closet
where you hang up your clothes.

C is for clown
with a funny red nose.

Dd Dd Dd

D is for dog
who follows you to school.

D is for diver
who dives in the pool.

D is for doormat
to wipe off your shoes.

D is for detective
who searches for clues.

Ee Ee Ee

E is for elbows
some dirty, some clean.

E is for eyes
that are blue, brown, or green.

E is for ears
that let you hear sound.

E is for earthworms
you find on the ground.

Ff Ff Ff

F is for flag
that waves in the breeze.

F is for fish
that swim in the seas.

F is for flashlight
to see in the dark.

F is for flowers
that grow in the park.

Gg Gg Gg

G is for gasoline
that makes your car go.

G is for garden
where vegetables grow.

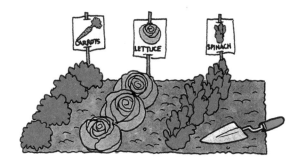

G is for gold
you find in a mine.

G is for grapes
that grow on a vine.

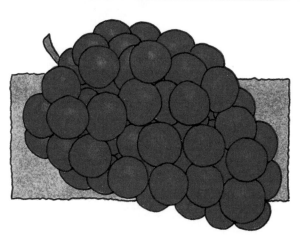

Hh Hh Hh

H is for helicopter
that flies overhead.

H is for headboard
attached to your bed.

H is for hot dog
you eat with a bun.

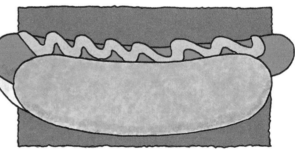

H is for horse
that gallops and runs.

Ii Ii Ii Ii Ii

I is for ice cube
that melts in your glass.

I is for instructor
who teaches the class.

I is for icing
you spread on a cake.

I is for igloo
the Eskimo makes.

Jj Jj Jj Jj

J is for jewelry
some made of gold.

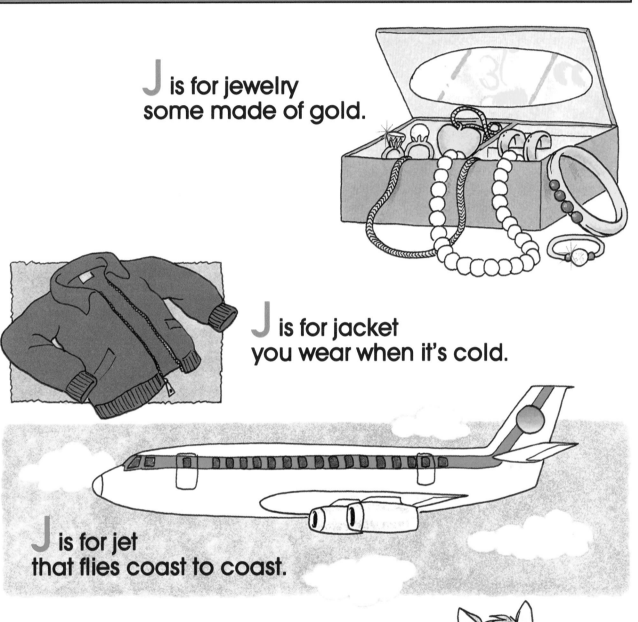

J is for jacket
you wear when it's cold.

J is for jet
that flies coast to coast.

J is for jelly
you spread on your toast.

Kk Kk Kk

K is for kitten
you hold in your hand.

K is for king
who rules the land.

K is for key
for unlocking a door.

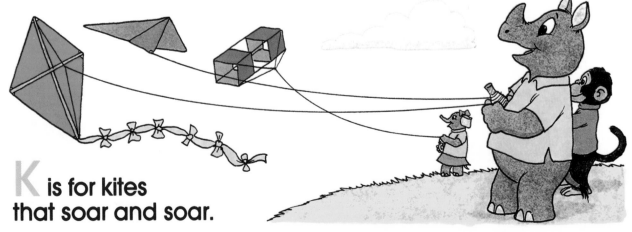

K is for kites
that soar and soar.

Ll Ll Ll Ll Ll

L is for legs
that bend at the knees.

L is for leaves
that fall from the trees.

L is for ladder
for climbing up high.

L is for laces
you learn how to tie.

Mm Mm Mm

M is for mailman
who brings you the mail.

M is for monkey
who swings by his tail.

M is for milk
you drink from a glass.

M is for mouse
who scoots through the grass.

Nn Nn Nn

N is for napkin
you place on your lap.

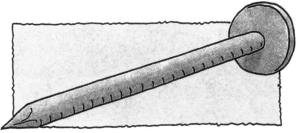

N is for nail
you tap, tap, tap.

N is for nurse
who cares for the sick.

N is for noodles
some thin, some thick.

Oo Oo Oo

O is for oars
to paddle a boat.

O is for otter
with a thick, furry coat.

O is for oranges
you pick from a tree.

O is for octopus
who lives in the sea.

Pp Pp Pp

P is for painting
you hang on the wall.

P is for pumpkins
some big, some small.

P is for pockets
to hold many things.

P is for parrot
with colorful wings.

Qq Qq Qq

Q is for quilt
you lay on your bed.

Q is for queen
with a crown on her head.

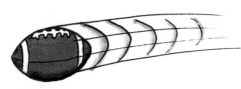

Q is for quarterback
who passes the ball.

Q is for quartet
that performs at the hall.

Rr Rr Rr

R is for radish
that grows in the ground.

R is for rabbit
that hops all around.

R is for raindrops
that fall on your head.

R is for rake
that you keep in the shed.

Ss Ss Ss

S is for stars
that shine in the night.

S is for supper
you eat every night.

S is for stairs
you climb up and down.

S is for signs
you see around town.

Tt Tt Tt

T is for textbooks
you study in school.

EARTH SCIENCE
ART
BIOLOGY
SOCIAL STUDIES
GEOGRAPHY
ARITHMETIC
HISTORY
ENGLISH

T is for towels
you lay by the pool.

T is for trees
that line the street.

T is for toast
that's good to eat.

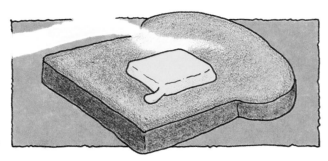

Uu Uu Uu

U is for umbrella
that protects you from rain.

U is for uniforms
some fancy, some plain.

U is for usher
who shows you your seat.

U is for utensils
you use when you eat.

Vv Vv Vv

V is for violin
you play with a bow.

V is for vegetables
that are fun to grow.

V is for volleyball
you play with a net.

V is for valentines
you like to get.

Ww Ww Xx Xx

 W is for wheels
that turn round and round.

 W is for whistle
that makes a loud sound.

X is for xylophone
to play a melody.

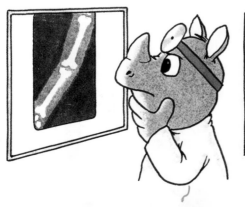

 X is for x-rays
the doctor must see.

Yy Yy Zz Zz

Y is for yard
where children can play.

Y is for youngsters
that grow everyday.

Z is for zoo
where you'll see many shows.

Z is for zippers
that open and close.

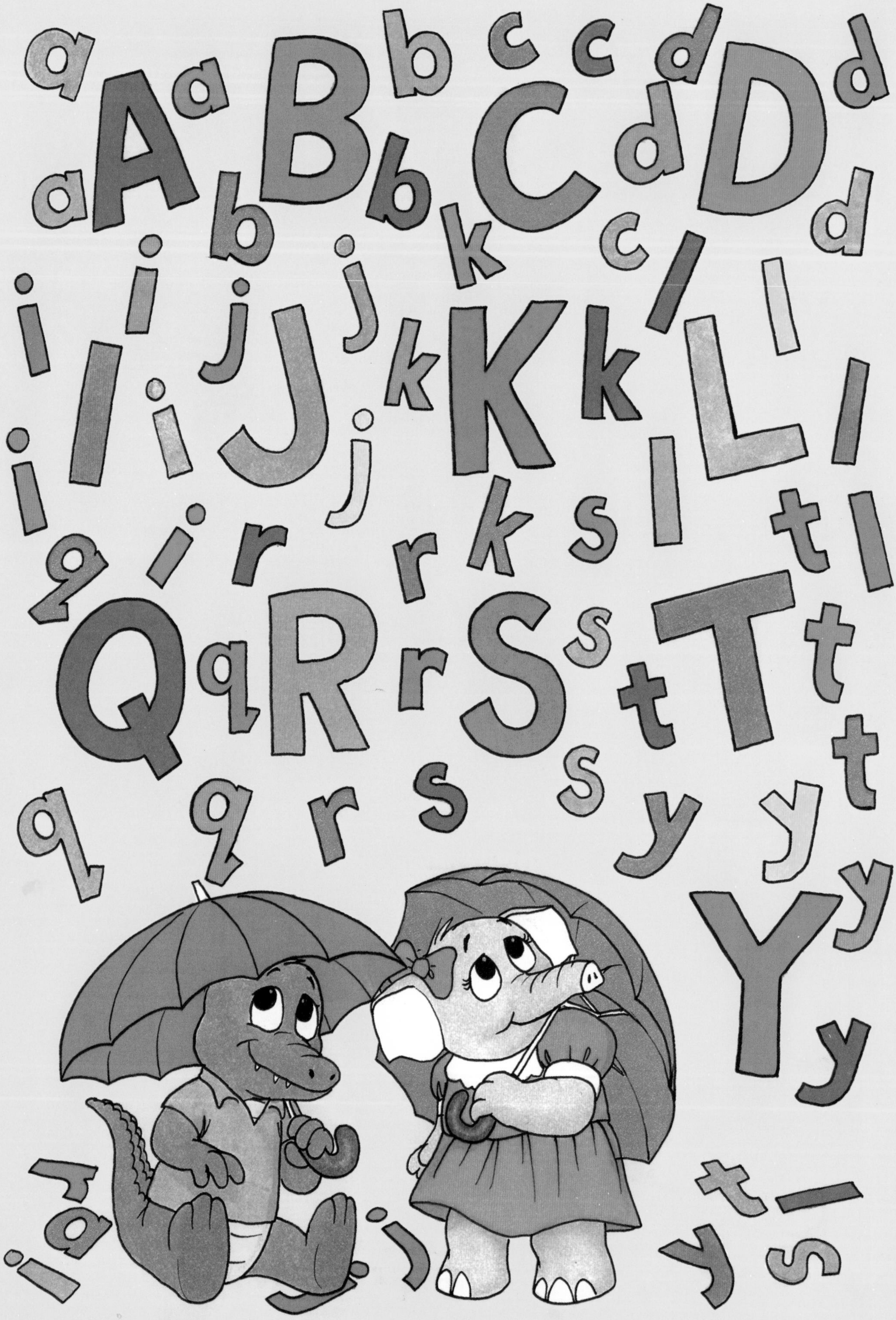